MANAGE RELATIONSHIPS MANAGE LIFE

8 Steps To Building & Maintaining Healthy Relationships

By

Ray Baker

Manage Relationships, Manage Life
Copyright © 2016 Ray Baker

Printed in the United States of America
First Edition Printing

Design by
Arbor Services, Inc.
http://www.arborservices.co/

ISBN: 978-0-692-69893-8
1. Title   2. Author   3. Relationships

Table of Contents

Foreword

This book is for anyone who wants to improve the relationships in their life.

In our lives, we have a vast number of relationships. We have relationships with our friends, our parents, our spouse or significant other, our children, our jobs, our bosses, our coworkers, and the list goes on and on. We have dozens of different relationships ever evolving each day. Are you successfully managing the relationships in your life? As Ray Baker explains in this informative and easy-to-read book, the bottom line to managing healthy relationships begins with you!

In this book, Ray underscores effective communication as the fundamental key to maintaining successful relationships and as a two-way street rooted in active listening. This is a skill which takes practice and some patience, and one which Ray teaches with both humor and examples.

This book is crammed full of good and practical information that will help you not only to improve but also to have productive relationships by teaching you first to understand before seeking to be understood. With clear and concise advice, Ray effectively reveals the healthy way to realistically manage your relationship expectations and limitations.

The road we travel through our lives is never paved smoothly. It is constantly winding, and oftentimes we are forced to change direction. As you use the tools and examples in this book, you will learn to be better prepared for managing those changes more effectively. It is said, "When the lesson is ready to be learned, the teacher will appear." If you are holding this book in your hand, the lesson is ready to be learned, and your teacher, Ray Baker, has appeared.

- Jim Cullum,
hypnosis consultant, personal coach,
and author of *Let Me Show You How I Love You*

Chapter One
The Assessment

We live in a world today where most people will experience relationship problems, be it spousal, parental, or job related. It is not a matter of "if" but "when." Add to this the number of outside influences— from well-meaning friends to your maiden aunt offering up opinions on what you should be doing, should not be doing, and how you should or should not be doing it—coupled with the demands of daily life—kids add greatly to this if you have them—and mole hills become mountains overnight.

So is there any hope for having any type of successful relationship? Honestly? No. Successful relationships don't happen on "hope." In fact, they don't "happen" at all. They exist because you—yes YOU—are willing to put in the time and effort. Yes, this will take time

AND effort to build a successful relationship. And here is the funny part. Ready? You might want to sit down for this. That time and effort doesn't start with changing your suddenly unsupportive spouse who is absolutely no help whatsoever, and it doesn't start with magically making your lame parents who don't even know what LOL means suddenly cool or even getting your moronic boss to suddenly appreciate the brilliance of you. It starts, quite simply, with YOU.

Okay, I know what you are thinking. You are thinking, *Me? There is nothing wrong with me.* Well, your spouse is thinking the same and so are your parents and so is your moronic boss. Since it is doubtful, unless you have some secret superhero power, you have the capacity to change any of them, you do, however, have the capacity to change YOURSELF and in turn change your relationships with all the people in your life into successful and healthy ones.

Let's start with the most basic of skills—communication. Every person has this skill, but very few master, or even manage it. In fact, were communication likened to driving a car, most people would be swerving into oncoming traffic. (If you listen closely you can probably hear horns blaring in your general direction.)

You are probably thinking you are a great communicator because you talk all the time. That is actually a sure sign of a poor communicator. It means you are likely not saying anything, in other words, not communicating. People tend to talk in circles, expecting that everyone knows and entirely understands exactly what they mean. Once again, with the exception of those of you with superhero powers, that is not going to happen, and you are going to spend a lot of time being frustrated, angry, and misunderstood.

What to do? First—stop. Stop talking. Start listening. Believe it or not, listening, not talking, is the most essential key to successful communication. Listen and really hear the other person. Strive to make a wholehearted effort to understand what the other person is saying. Stop defending your position and start accepting the other person's. That is not to say you need to apologize and agree. On the contrary, simply acknowledge. Not only will you gain the other person's respect, more importantly, you will earn the other person's willingness to hear you. You will achieve a level of successful communication, and in so doing you will have mastered the first element in building a successful and healthy relationship.

All right, now that you have managed to stop talking (go on, pat yourself on the back), it is time to delve a little deeper into how you come across to others.

We all have baggage. (That is, assuming you are over the age of six. Yes, six. By seven, some boy or girl has left you out of his/her group valentine.) Baggage is like carbs: some is good and some is bad. Good baggage is what we have learned from, while bad baggage is what we are using against someone who had nothing to do with the original situation.

Is this sounding familiar? It ought to because we all do it until we make a conscious effort to stop. How? You closely examine the baggage, like cleaning out the closet. Do you have any use for it? (Trust me, you don't.) Is it serving any purpose? (Except for tainting your other relationships, probably not.) Does it still fit

your lifestyle? (Doubtful.) So why are you still holding onto it? Because it is easier to stash it than deal with it.

The problem with stashing it is you will continue to repeat the mistake, be it dating the same type of personality or staying stuck in the same job. Dealing with it means making a substantial change in your life to break a cycle that by now has become comfortable and familiar. But if you muster up your courage and look closely at your baggage, you will recognize two salient things: first, you are not an entirely innocent party, and second, you are not an entirely innocent party. (It bears repeating because you may have slipped a little on your listening skills.) Most baggage stems from jealousy, plain and simple. Jealousy is part of human nature, but it doesn't have to be a way of life. Jealousy stems more from you than from the other person. It denotes a sense of low self-worth. Why do you view yourself in such a low light? Okay, you're not Julia Roberts. (Trust me, when she gets up in the morning, neither is she.) So you aren't Derek Jeter. Okay, I admit, I have nothing for this one. The point is you are you. You have both good parts and bad parts, and all those parts make you who you are. However, if you are so focused on your own insecurities that you cannot recognize your own self-worth, you will fail to understand how someone else can recognize it, leaving you suspicious and distrustful, with an ever-present sense of jealousy.

Now I am not here to pour on the sugar and pin a medal to your chest for how wonderful you are. What I am here to do is teach you how to break down the barriers you have spent a lifetime (up until now) putting up, and get you to recognize (and cop to) your own role in the relationships in your life. I'm here to teach you how you can attain and maintain a level of general happiness in your life.

I warned you earlier, this will take time and effort. Yes, even being happy takes time and effort because (again assuming you are over the age of six) this is not as simple as it sounds. Agreed, it should be as simple as a big, sticky spool of cotton candy, but nearly every one of us has managed to make this simple act into one of the most complicated productions since *Madame Butterfly*.

Have you ever watched a dog chase his tail? He will spend hours chasing it until he catches it. But he cannot hold onto it, and he will spend hours chasing it until he catches it again. Like that dog, people live in a constant state of pursuit. We have come to rely on possessions or people to make us happy, and as a result, whatever happiness we manage is fleeting. We collect "things" and subsequently we accumulate baggage (you thought I'd forgotten about that, didn't you?).

Let's try an experiment. Choose a person who you trust without question, a person whose opinion is one you value. (This probably should not be your drinking buddy.)

Now, ask this person to honestly assess you. Some might be a bit hesitant in this role, although most will probably jump at the opportunity with all the enthusiasm of a kid in a candy store. Try not to take it personally. Yes, I know it is hard, but this is about change and growth to get you where you need to be in life, so swallow hard, smile, and be prepared to hear things that make you uncomfortable. The truth is seldom pleasant. It downright hurts, but it is a good hurt. It's like when you were a child and your favorite pair of shoes suddenly fit too tight. You outgrew them and it was time to grow into a new pair, so you experienced growing pains. This is not a bad hurt. You were growing and you are still growing.

Now that that brave person has duly assessed you, it is time for you to acknowledge and process what you have heard. (No, you do not get to seek out your drinking buddy.) Don't be afraid to consider the probability that you have carved out a distinct pattern of behavior, a set lifestyle that has resulted in some unattractive habits, which has led to some unhealthy relationships.

Now for the really hard part—change. Change is scary. Nobody likes change, but without change nothing happens. Without change there cannot be progress. You cannot do the same things and expect different results. There is something to be said for the road less traveled because it is far more dangerous to travel the same path in life than to take a new direction out of fear.

Fear is paralyzing and polarizing. It is also false. It is an imagined pattern of thinking that prevents us from acting. (Okay, yes, our fear should dictate that skiing a black diamond trail after one lesson on the bunny hill is not wise.) But people tend to allow fear to dictate everyday decisions, and subsequently they hold onto (here comes that word again) baggage. Fear dictates moving into a new house, changing jobs, even getting out of a bad relationship.

Ask yourself these two simple questions: One, what do I want? Two, how do I get it? (I said they were simple questions; I did not say they had simple answers.) You cannot merely sit on your couch and "imagine." If it were as simple as that, megamillions would be paid out on a weekly basis. You have to be proactive, to work for what you want. Change does not happen because you want it; it happens because you cause it. You have to let go of the past. You cannot embrace the future if your arms are holding crap.

However, fear not, take heart, there is hope. If you are willing to make a true and conscious effort to halt your current mode of behavior, if you can take off your blinders and let yourself become aware of your established patterns, and—and this is the big one— you are willing to break those patterns (you have to want it), you can achieve genuine happiness in each of the relationships in your life.

Chapter Two
The Opportunity

Now that you have been duly assessed, you are probably wondering how in the heck you make change. Where are you supposed to start? It is all so overwhelming. Yes, but it does not have to be. Remember, this is not about making your life perfect or making perfect relationships. Life wasn't meant to work that way. Life is a challenge. A challenge will strengthen you; a fight will weaken you.

This is about helping you effectively (key word) manage the relationships in your life—all of them. What people tend to forget is all relationships, be they spousal, familial, friendship, or business, have one thing in common. They each revolve around one important and shared element—YOU. How you manage any given relationship will directly impact the others.

You doubt? Okay, you have had a bad day at work. Nothing went right. The computers were down, the printer jammed, your boss blamed you for a colleague's error, leading you to confront the colleague who could not have cared less, and there was only decaf coffee. It was just a miserable day, and to boot, you got stuck in a rubbernecking traffic jam for twenty-five minutes on the way home. Finally, you get home. The dog is so happy to see you he runs up and jumps on you. You snap at him, telling him to get down, and then snap at your spouse who snapped at you for snapping at the dog.

The day just keeps getting better and better, doesn't it? That is because you did not effectively manage one relationship, and it is impacting another. It is a trickle-down effect, like a leak. Where you see water coming out is not the leak; it is only the effect. You need to find the source of the leak and effectively repair or manage it.

A stressful situation at work turned into a stressful situation at home because you failed to manage your position. One directly influenced the other. To be fair, stress is difficult to manage. Everybody thinks they manage it just fine, but truthfully hardly anybody does. That is because stress is *reactive*, and to manage it effectively, you need to be *proactive.*

Like carbs and baggage, there is good stress and bad stress. Good stress energizes, while bad stress exhausts. Few stressful situations are a surprise, which is a good thing, because each has a deciphered pattern that allows for clear-cut ways to adjust. So in that instance where an unexpected stressful situation creeps up, your auto response is proactive.

How does this happen? It is easier than you think. (Trust me here.) It is as simple as turning a phrase. Let's go back to the work situation. *Reactive*: you initiated a confrontation with your colleague, which put you both in a defensive position. When two parties are each in a defensive position, neither party is L I S T E N I N G. If you are not listening, then you are not communicating; and if you are not communicating, you cannot manage the relationship.

Now *proactive*: you did not approach your colleague from a confrontational standpoint, but rather with a genuine desire to understand his position. You take the offense, you L I S T E N, you have a dialogue, and you manage the relationship.

Are you reminded of the idiom, "The best defense is a good offense"? It is more than a sports catchphrase; it is a simple (not simplistic; do not be confused) ideal that has wielded more influence in more political arenas than all the blustering echoed on Capitol Hill.

Consider those times in your own life when you have taken control of a situation by shouting (by being on the defense). Did you accomplish an effective resolution? Of course you didn't. You were likely met with resistance (an opposing defense) because (and this will come as a real shock to you) you did not have control of the situation. You were not in the position to effectively manage the relationship at that particular moment.

It is like two magnets: two negatives will always be opposed; they will never connect, while one positive with one negative will hold a strong connection. You need to assess which you are and which you want to be.

Chapter Three
Step One: Know Yourself

Self-examination is hard. This is most likely the reason most people do not do it. It is so much easier to assume (you all know what happens when you do that, right?) the fault is with the other person rather than admitting there might be even the slightest, most remote possibility it might be you.

Now here is the funny part about that. If every person were to be correct about it being "the other person" (do you see what's coming here?), every person would be the other person. Are you scratching your head? It is a simple, basic truth. It's like the old adage, "If you are not part of the solution, you are part of the problem." That doesn't just apply to primary elections, defensive driving, and jury duty. It applies to everyday life, and it all starts with you. If you are not part of the solution in your own life, you are part—the biggest part, mind you—of the problem.

So, now that we have that straight, who are you? Do you know? Okay, the resounding answers here are deafening, but you are not your career. And, before you sound off again, no, you are not Leon's mom or Phoebe's husband, and you are most definitely not Janelle's bff. Those are associated roles; and that bff one, yeah, that one tends to generally be temporary.

Clearly, this is going to take some serious work, so, if you'll pardon the quote, "Fasten your seatbelts, it's going to be a bumpy ride."

Who you are is based on a deeper but not entirely more complex connection to two things. The first is how you project yourself to others, because to a great degree you will become what you believe. The second is the perception others have of you. While the first is an ideal you wholly control, the second is an ideal others will form of you based on a number of mitigating factors from how you look and who you associate with to what religion you practice and even your social media presence.

While these two ideals may, at first glance, seem unrelated, they are intricately connected because, quite simply, by controlling the first—and recognizing and understanding who you are—you dispel any misconceptions drawn by the second. (You might want to take a minute to check your recent Facebook posts.) Okay, so without psychoanalyzing, let's have a look at you. What are your strengths? What are your weaknesses? How do you control them? Or, more importantly, how do they control you? Oh yes, I am sorry to have to tell you, but your strengths and your weaknesses both very much control you. Your strengths lend themselves to a confidence that in some instances borders on arrogance, while your weaknesses lend themselves to timidity that can border on fear.

While an excess of either is unhealthy, a balance of both is necessary for healthy checks and balances for knowing exactly who you are. You can then utilize the benefits of this knowledge because, as the saying goes, knowledge is power.

Now, how you use that power is what will define who you are and dispel who you are not. For example, if you are naturally confident but you use that confidence to beat down those around you, you are a bully. Whether you are a gifted eight-year-old hitter on his Little League team or a brilliantly foresighted forty-year-old in the boardroom, you are allowing your strength to control you. In so doing, your strength becomes a weakness because it will lend to you perceiving yourself based on one particular trait or behavior pattern.

You are thinking, *Well, I can't help it if I'm smarter than everybody else around me. That's who I am. If they can't keep up, that's on them, not me.* Wrong. It is on you. If your strength brings out other people's weaknesses, then your strength is a strength you cannot manage and thus is a weakness. If that eight-year-old Little Leaguer cannot play well with others, the game is lost. The same rule applies in later life.

Human nature being what it is, we all like to toot our own horn. We all look for that nod of acknowledgment for whatever accomplishment we've managed, and when we don't get it, we create it for ourselves. That is okay, to a degree. It is fine to be proud, but it becomes a problem, or unmanageable, when you allow it to morph into an air of self-importance.

And human nature being what it is, we all like to hide our weaknesses. We all look to disguise the chink in the armor. That, too, is okay, to a degree. It is logical to disguise a weakness or an insecurity but, again, to a degree. If in your attempt to disguise your own weakness, you spotlight somebody else's, you are allowing your weakness to become a false strength.

In both these instances your strength and your weakness control you. You fail to recognize them and thereby you fail to understand them with any degree of knowledge.

As a rule, people tend to hide their true selves. We put forth who we think the other person wants to see rather than risk revealing who we truly are. That *best foot forward* rule Mom worked so hard to instill in each of us is a little misleading. Yes, you should work to make a good first impression but not to the extent it is a false first impression.

It is fair enough to say most people are not intentionally deceitful, but rather it becomes partially

unintentional out of a desire to be accepted because
we all have a fear of rejection. I say *partially* because
we all know when we are acting out of character. We
can *feel* it even if we don't admit it, and while we can
live this pretense for a while—some of us longer than
others—sooner or later the pretense breaks down.
While who you truly are may not surface, who people
perceive you to be will.

This is especially true in the early stages of
romantic relationships, which I humorously refer to
as the lying phase. Consider that little white lie about
being a huge sci-fi fan. What could it harm, right?
Your new love is perfect in every other way. So what
if he/she collects all the toys and so what if they never
stop talking about movie plotlines. You sat through
Star Wars and survived. How good for you . . . and
then came the ComicCon. And suddenly you find
yourself annoyed, but who are you annoyed with? No,
not the other person. Look deeper. You are annoyed
with yourself. You are just taking it out on the other
person who now has no idea who you are because
YOU have no idea.

It is equally true in business relationships. You start a new job and you want to fit in so you agree with the general water cooler opinion on whatever the topic of the day is; could be politics, could be the *Dancing with the Stars* finale. You chime right in with the tide of popular opinion. Eventually, though, especially as relates to politics—which, by the way, is generally a good topic to avoid discussing—your own opinion surfaces and the real you is revealed. Again, you are left feeling annoyed, and again it is not with anybody else. It is just easier to *pretend* (see how that word keeps popping up) so.

Simply put, happiness should not be a moving target. It should not be based on things or other people, and it should not shift with the changing tide. A new car won't make you happy for longer than it takes that new car smell to dissipate, and a new relationship won't do it either. If you do not know who you are, you cannot know what you want. Knowing who you are will help you define and articulate your happiness—for yourself and *then* to someone else. Not the other way around.

You cannot look to someone or something else for your own happiness. It won't last. If you don't know what you are looking for, how can you expect to find it in someone/something else? That's just "filler"— empty calories. It won't sustain you, and until you can recognize satisfaction in yourself, you will see dissatisfaction with everything else.

We have all grown up with labels: the smart one, the funny one, the pretty one. Parents label children; teachers label students; friends, colleagues, and spouses even label each other; and, this is the sad part, we label ourselves. We comfortably wear an old label, or worse, we slip on a copycat label so we can fit into our own circle. We spend half our life imitating celebrities, athletes, and each other because it is easier to fit in than to stand out.

We spend more time getting to know the cast of the newest reality television show than we spend getting to know ourselves. Why is that? Why is it so hard for us to face who we are? Because, as stated early on, self-examination is hard. It requires a level of honesty we are not comfortable administering. It is easier to wear one label at home, another at work, and another with friends than it is to peel them all off and get to know our own core essence. Because what if we don't like who we are?

That would be okay; in fact, that would be ideal. It would mean you have delved into your very being and recognized there is work to be done. It would mean you have taken stock and are ready to understand your history and to take control of your strengths and your weaknesses and recognize who you really are.

Listen, the plain truth is none of us is perfect, and none of us will ever be perfect. No amount of work, therapy, or self-examination will change that. This is not about being perfect. This is about getting you to do two things: summoning the courage to recognize you have work to do, and giving you the tools to get you to do it so you can maintain and manage healthy relationships. Start with the single most important relationship you will ever have, the only one which will ever truly allow for the others to exist.

Chapter Four
Step Two: Do Your Homework

We've all heard the old quote about failing to learn from the past or repeating the past or being doomed by the past. Whatever wording you prefer, the message is clear. The past —your past—can either help you or hurt you, teach you or taunt you; it is entirely up to you.

Your past is the best indicator you have of your future, but only if you use it correctly. Can you learn from your mistakes? You can if you recognize them, and that cannot be emphasized enough. You must be able to recognize the mistakes of your own past in order to avoid repeating them. You are not tied to your past—not last year, not the last hour.

You need to do your homework. This is key in building and maintaining healthy relationships. You must know your own history and understand it, why you do what you do, why you make the same mistakes, because only with this innate understanding will you be able to understand the other person's history as you work toward building a healthy relationship. If you cannot understand your own unhealthy patterns, you will not only fail to understand the other person's, but moreover, you will continue to forge unhealthy relationships.

Just as you need to understand your own history, you will need to understand the other person's before diving into a relationship. Because just as you are prone to repeating unhealthy but ingrained patterns, so likely is the other person. That is not to say people cannot change; of course they can, but they have to *want* to, and you have to be able to recognize the difference.

People tend to ignore the warning signs—and there are *always* warning signs. We all give off little, and sometimes not so little, clues, and all with the hope nobody will notice; and most times nobody does. How many times have you said (after the fact), "I

didn't know?" Yes, you did, deep down you absolutely did, but you didn't want to see it so you *chose* to not know because you did not *want* to know. Too often we become so enamored by another person, job, or situation, we ignore the warning bells. Bad habits (jobs or situations) don't suddenly "crop up"; you need to pay attention to your own barometer.

Imagine going to a bank for a loan. You look like a nice person; you are polite and well spoken. You are attractive with a nice smile. You are even a bit funny. Yep, you're a keeper all right, but does that mean you're walking out with the money? Do you really think the loan officer is going to hand over a check without looking at your background? Of course not. He is going to look at your past credit performance to gauge your future credit performance.

Well, our relationships are the biggest investments we can make, yet we don't bother to do relationship credit reports. Instead we forge full steam ahead, and when the bad habits "suddenly" crop up, we have the nerve to act surprised. Or worse yet, we lament, "I thought I could change him/her/it." Really?

Pretend for a minute you have met someone who is divorced because they admit having cheated. Does this mean they will cheat on you? Maybe, maybe not. You need to be able to understand their history. You need to be able to decipher if there is a pattern in this history. That does not mean you need to hire a private investigator and call up all the exes. It means you have to be smart and listen, really l i s t e n to how the other person talks of their past. Has every relationship ended for the same reason? Does he excuse his behavior by blaming the other person? Is she always the victim in the story?

Now pretend for a minute that same person makes the same admission, but rather than make excuses and place blame, he state right out his fault. Instead of treating it with nonchalance, he instead treats it as an epiphany into understanding his own history.

Do you see the two distinct patterns and, more importantly, how each is a good indicator toward performance of future relationships?

What would you do if, after a few weeks of "togetherness," you suggest meeting each other's friends? The other person shoots down the idea. She doesn't have time for friends, and at the mention of family she states that everyone in her family is crazy, better to be disconnected. This is a loud warning bell that too many people will miss because most people themselves are disconnected. The same is true of that new job. If the boss interviewing you is angry, overbearing, and tells you he hopes you will fare better than the last four people in the last three months, that is a loud bell you are going to be miserable at that job.

People don't talk to each other anymore. You can't spot the warning signs from the screen of your smart phone. There is no tone in a text and, wonderful as it might be for reconnecting with your best friend from fifth grade, social media cannot replace good, old-fashioned human interaction.

Do you know where the person you just met comes from? (And don't say Brooklyn.) Do you know what motivates them, what they are passionate about, what pushes them over the edge? You don't, do you? And you think that is okay because you'll just figure it out as you go, right?

Okay, let's go with that theory. You and your new person have had a blissful three weeks and then he vanishes. No e-mail reply, no returned texts. Nothing. He even unfriended you. What happened? The last thing you remember is talking about how our military doesn't belong overseas. It's enough already. It's a fight we can't win—and it's not even our fight—and it's a debt our children's great-grandchildren will be paying. It's just so stupid.

Did you know the other person comes from a fiercely proud and actively serving military family? No, you did not because you did not bother to learn where the other person comes from. Would you have changed your position? No, of course not, but you would have changed how you approached it to avoid causing any intentional hurt to the other person.

A relationship background check isn't about playing private investigator, it is about learning about the other person so you can avoid tripping the minefields. It's about becoming aware and learning to delicately approach and manage uncomfortable situations.

All right, let's trust that you understand your own history enough to know where you come from. How do you understand another person's? You do that by listening to both what they are saying and, even more importantly, what they are not saying. You have to ask questions and pay attention to the answers. We all have a tendency to hear what we want to hear and not what is being said. (By turnaround, we all have the tendency to say what we suspect the other person wants to hear.) This is because—are you ready?—we like the comfort zone.

Why not just ignore history and move on to the future? The past is the past, right? What is done is done, right? Yes, that's right, but if you don't work to understand it, it becomes your future. Yeah, but you can't unring a bell, can you? No, you can't, but you can learn to not keep ringing the same bell.

In order to have healthy relationships you have to plan, you have to prepare. Most people will put more planning into buying a new car than forming a new relationship. Go on, admit it, this is you. You read all the advertisements for weeks, you research all the new models, and you shop a dozen different dealers, all with a fixed cost in mind. You make a plan. You are prepared.

Don't the relationships in your life deserve the same effort? Of course they do, because be it a job, spouse, or friend, you are going to have that relationship in your life a lot longer—or one would hope—than that black convertible coupe.

Chapter Five
Step Three: Set Realistic Expectations

Think for a moment about the most important relationship in your life right now and all the expectations you had for how wonderful it would be. It could be your spouse or a longtime friend or even your kids because, for purposes of the question, it is not the relationship that matters, it is the answer to the question.

None of them have worked out quite exactly as you imagined, have they? Oh sure, there have been more good days than bad, but why haven't they worked out quite exactly the way you imagined? You can't guess? It is because you projected expectations that were likely unrealistic. You expected every day would be as happy as the day you said "I do," and you couldn't possibly ever imagine regretting those two words (yeah, you have). How could you and that longtime friend ever be at each other's throats, and the kids . . .? It's okay to admit it, the first time little Timmy drew with a crayon on the wall you instinctively hollered at him.

What went wrong? Nothing, at least not with the spouse, friend, or kids. What went wrong was your expectations of those relationships. You projected specific expectations of what each of those relationships would be and then expected all involved to magically live up to them.

Expectations cannot be set in a relationship, not the way you are most likely setting them. You need to turn it around. Rather than going into a relationship—any relationship—with specific expectations for what that relationship will be, you need to go into it with expectations for what it will not be. In other words, you need to use everything you have learned about yourself (you thought you were going to get a pass on that chapter, didn't you?) to understand what you don't want so you can then set realistic expectations for maintaining what you do want. (Are you seeing the recurring theme?) To borrow on the phrase, you cannot keep doing the same thing the same way and expect different results.

What you can do is work to develop a sense of trust in your relationships to define your expectations within fair and realistic boundaries. Identify your expectations to both yourself and the other party and know the limitations. Avoid expecting perfection; it will lead to disappointment. Start separating what you *want* from what you *need*.

If you are thinking those two words are interchangeable, you are not alone and you are not entirely mistaken. However, you need to recognize that while at times they may be similar, there are distinct differences between the two words.

You may want a fourteen-room, six-bedroom, five-bath Victorian home with nine-foot ceilings and six-foot windows? Unless you are part of the Gates family, it's probably not needed. A solid home with good insulation, sound indoor plumbing, and ample closet space is more likely what you need. That Victorian, grand though it might be, is an unrealistic expectation and classifies as a want, while that solid home is a real expectation of what you need.

We treat the people in our lives in much the same manner, leading to the single most common detriment to any relationship. We come to have such specific images of our relationships and what we *think* we want, we expel an inordinate amount of effort and energy into pigeonholing them to fit that image instead of making allowances for what they are.

In other words, we work to mold our relationships to be something other than what they are instead of managing the limitations.

Does that mean you have to settle for mediocracy or make excuses? No, just the opposite. It means you need to redefine your expectations. What allowances or exceptions can you live with, and which can you live without? That sports fanatic you married isn't going to suddenly give up the crush of Sunday games for leisurely champagne brunches, and that longtime couch potato friend isn't going to cruise the Caribbean on a whim because you want to. Little Timmy may never be that perfect little angel, and you should not expect anything different.

What you should do is recognize each relationship for what it is and be aware of the limitations. Ask yourself, can I accept them? Do not look at any relationship in your life with the expectation of changing it, but rather look at every relationship with the preparedness for managing the limitations accordingly and the expectations realistically.

Once you have learned to identify what you truly want and need, you will develop an acute manner for not only spotting the limitations within the key relationships in your life but more importantly a keen ability for managing them.

Chapter Six
Step Four: Communicate Effectively

Let's pause here a moment to revisit a key element in chapter one, communication. Yes, I know, you are thinking, *Why?* Yes, I can hear the whining, and don't you dare turn the page. We need to now look at a different level of communicating, and yes, there are different levels.

Consider the last disagreement you had with someone, anyone. Maybe it was a parent, a sibling, a spouse, friend, colleague, whomever, it likely left you feeling frustrated and maybe even downright angry. Now, hours or (although let us hope not) days later, you are still frustrated, but when that person (because they have moved past this point of contention) or even someone entirely uninvolved (because they have no idea why you are in a mood) asks you what's wrong, what do you say? That's right, you say, "Nothing."

You shut down and shut out the other person. You completely retreat—almost. *Almost* because your body language is most certainly betraying this stoic stance you are posturing. You are likely as rigid as an army private, with your arms crossed and your jaw tight. You get the picture.

Rather than communicating your feelings, you sever the connection, not the relationship. Mind you, there is a difference, but a connection. This will pass, but there will be a scar; it is called a grudge, and the first chance you get, you are going to wield it like a sword. Not good, not good at all.

That is classic unhealthy communication, and while it is common, it is not genuine and is not the way healthy relationships are managed. Healthy communication exists on an honesty that allows for genuine expression.

Have you ever watched couples who are married for a long period of time? There is an easiness about them that is more than their being "used to each other."

That easiness stems from their ability to honestly, *genuinely,* communicate with one another, which, by the way, then trickles down to their being able to do it with everybody else in their life.

This is not a difficult skill to learn or master, but it is a skill that is being suffocated by technology. That is not to say that BlackBerries and iPads and all the other modern technology is solely responsible for the decline of society as a social entity, but it does get a big part of the credit.

And to be clear, conversation is not the same as communication. Conversation relates to talking *to* each other in an expression of opinion, while communication relates to talking *with* each other in an expression of feelings. If you just asked, "What's the difference?" you need to put down your iPhone and go back to the beginning because clearly you have not been *listening.* Oh . . . right . . . *listening, l i s t e n i n g.*

That is why that long-married couple made it past the third anniversary; they know how to *listen* to one another. They pay attention, they can *read* each other because sometimes you are saying more than you realize by what you are not saying in that your body, from the tilt of your head to the positioning of your feet, can express more about what you are feeling than your words.

Think a minute about a dog wagging his tail. Friendly, right? You should go over and pet him. Should you, really? Are his ears up or back? Are his teeth showing? (No, he is not smiling.) Is any part of his upper body lowered? These are all signs you should definitely not only not pet him but you should move away slowly.

People use body language (sometimes subtle, sometimes not so subtle) to give off similar signs to express what they are feeling but are unable or unwilling to say. And although most times misinterpreting those signs won't land you in the ER, you still need to be able to read them if you expect to manage a fully healthy relationship.

Like any other skill, effective communication takes time to learn. But unlike those four year of high school French, it is a skill you can rely on for doing two vitally important things in your efforts for maintaining healthy relationships: *talking* and *listening* with an honesty in what you are saying and with a genuine understanding for what you are hearing.

Don't hear only the words but the emotion being projected both by you and by the other person. Be aware of the signs, be in control of the signals you are sending out, and be receptive to the signals you are getting back. The old line about "actions speak(ing) louder than words" will mark whether your relationship is healthy or unhealthy.

Remember, you might be the one doing the talking, but you are not the only one who might be saying something.

Chapter Seven
Step Five: Get Intimate

While communication is key in any healthy relationship, it cannot exist without intimacy. (Okay, before you get too excited here, do not confuse intimacy with *intimacy*.) Intimacy in communication is wholly different from romantic intimacy, but make no mistake, it is no less important.

Have you ever wondered what sustains a relationship that has absolutely no romantic ties and yet exhibits a closeness you—in *all* your romantic relationships— have never had? You guessed it, very good, yes, intimacy! There is a closeness, a bond, rooted in any number of things, not the least of which is *caring*. A whole and deep caring not just about the person. You care about your neighbor, right? You wouldn't want to see them hit by a bus or anything, but it's doubtful you share any level of intimacy with them. No, this level of caring goes to the heart, or more precisely, what touches the other person's heart.

Everyone, every child, every old person, you, me, we all have that one element which defines us. Not the label, not the reputation, not any of that, but that one crucial element that cuts deep within us, that one element we could never be without in life.

Whatever it is, it is what lies centermost to the other person's heart. If you can hold an understanding—a true and real understanding—of this aspect of who they are, you will reach a level of intimacy that will solidify your relationship and hold it strong.

This is not something that can be faked. You cannot pretend to care. You are probably thinking, *Well, what if I don't care all that much? Can I help how I feel?* In this case, no, you can't, but you can help your relationship by truly working to understand why the other person does.

When you can recognize why something that doesn't mean too much to you means the world to another person—and honestly understand *why*—then you will have developed a level of intimacy that will sustain a healthy relationship. You do not have to learn to like something you do not like; you simply have to care enough about the other person to take the time to learn why they do.

It is easy to dismiss what another person values or to make light of it. You don't mean to do it, but you don't understand it, you don't care about it, you have no interest in it, you dismiss it. But what if there are deeper reasons than the obvious?

Maybe the sports fanatic who never takes you to brunch for fear of missing any minute of any Sunday game has a deeper reason than the obvious. Maybe their mom took them to their first game and every game she could manage, and watching those games reconnects a nostalgia otherwise lost.

Maybe it reminds them of a childhood connection and the life lessons learned on and off the field. Maybe it rekindles in them a recollection of times when race and ethnicity didn't matter because everyone made up a part of the team and it just felt good to be accepted without being judged.

Or, okay, maybe they just plain love sports.

Whatever the reason, whether it becomes a point of contention or connection between you is up to you. If you are willing to take the time to learn about and understand this pivotal element and you can put aside your own views long enough to consider the other person's, you manage a level of intimacy all healthy relationships need to survive.

So, is your relationship doomed if you don't learn to love sports even after you understand why the other person does? Are you still going to have to learn all the players' names and what numbers they wear? Do you now have to memorize the team mascots? Of course not. This is not about teaching you to fake it; it can't be done.

You cannot fake what you do not feel and still expect to maintain a healthy relationship. You don't need to love the game, even after coming to understand why the other person does; you need only to let them love it. You need do nothing more than let them know they can trust you enough with whatever it is that speaks to their heart—and for whatever reason—and you will be okay with that.

So relax. You don't have to change your opinion, you don't have to spend Sundays on the couch shouting at the television or pretending to share the other person's passion.

Intimacy, at its core, is trust, and trust carries with it a little hint of vulnerability, but it also carries with it a quiet strength drawn from absolute honesty. To be vulnerable is to be open without pretense. To reach intimacy on a genuine level, you have to be willing to be a little vulnerable to allow for getting to a level of pure caring all healthy relationships exist on.

This level of intimacy is so key to keeping your relationship strong, and yet it remains the most overlooked. People have no patience, no tolerance for things of no interest to them. Yet, people all expect that everything of interest to them, everything they value to be treated with the same regard, and when it is not there is seldom any discussion. Communication—verbal communication, because nonverbal communication is most definitely being expressed—is pushed aside but not without doing some small but irrevocable damage.

Be aware, be genuine, and be intimate in your relationships, all your relationships. Avoid treating the other person like a social media post with a cute and quick "like" as you scroll down. If you expect to hold truly healthy relationships, you will need to take time to nurture this level of real intimacy.

Chapter Eight
Step Six: Be Thoughtful

Look around now at the relationships in your life. Are you generous toward them? If your impulse answer related in any way to your holiday gift-giving generosity, we need to talk. You need to pay close attention, but okay, let's start with your gift giving.

How do you buy that other person a gift? Do you buy it with *them* in mind or with *you* in mind? For example: you see a shirt, you buy it, and you give it to the other person. Do you say, "I bought this shirt for you to wear," or do you say, "I saw this shirt and thought you might like it"? Yes, I know, you always mean the latter (it's okay, I know), but you always say the first. You didn't think of the other person when you bought the shirt. You thought of yourself because your reason for buying it was your wanting to see the other person in it. Yes, yes, your underlying reason was that they would like it, but your primary reason was all about you. You wanted to think you were acting to please the other person, but really you acted to please yourself. Whether or not the other person liked the shirt was irrelevant; you wanted them to wear it because you liked it.

Now don't feel bad. It's a good bet the other person bought your last gift for the same reason, and it's these selfish, albeit unintended, behaviors that weaken an otherwise strong relationship.

Now, unintentional or not, it is an unhealthy mindset you need to change. You need to stop projecting what you want under the pretense of it being what you think the other person wants.

You don't think of yourself as a selfish person, right? Well, nobody does. We are all generous to a fault—big group pat on the back. Feel better? Yes, well, sadly, we are all selfish in any number of ways, from buying that shirt to asking what movie the other person wants to see and then declaring which movie we want to see as a decisive selection or any other situation so common to everyday life it's not even noticed.

This "I" mindset has become so ingrained it is second nature. Thinking of the other person first has taken on an unnatural fit; it doesn't feel comfortable. This is especially true in our romantic lives. We find a comfortable routine; sometimes it's a good balance, sometimes it's a one way street. It's all good, right?

No, wrong. It's not all good. It's the "I" mindset. If it were all good, you'd be asking questions. You would be exhibiting a show of generosity for putting the other person first, but that is an awkward position. It's more comfortable to assume you know what the other person likes than it is to *ask*. Just like that shirt or the movie. The "I" mindset has become an ingrained pattern.

All right now, maybe you are seeing a bit of yourself here, but it's not that big of a problem really. You can't please all of the people all of the time anyway, right? Yes, that's right, and this isn't about pleasing all of the people all of the time or even all of the people some of the time and so on. This is about learning to be a selfless person.

Being a selfless person is not about being a people pleaser. It is not about turning you into some ninny running around trying to make everybody else's life better. You'd be popping Valium like aspirin the first month.

Rather, this is about getting you to stop, to think about your actions as it relates to another person. There is nothing wrong with knowing what you want and what you don't want or what you like and what you don't like as long as the same holds true about the other person. Do you know what they want or don't want or like or don't like? The most expensive gift in the world is worthless if given without thought for the person receiving it.

The same is true for giving of ourselves—our emotional giving. How generous are you in that department? Are you emotionally available? How much of yourself do you give? When another person is talking, are you hurrying them along so you can get on to something else, someplace else to be, something else to do? Or are you tuning out, just waiting for them to finish so you can speak? Or are you putting together in your own mind what you will say back? It's little habits like this, seemingly so insignificant, that pose the biggest dangers. This type of passive selfishness can leave us so entrenched in our own positions, it escalates even the smallest matter.

By comparison, the reverse is equally true for there being healthy selfish behavior, *me* time. It is okay, even essential, to managing a healthy relationship to tell the other person you need some downtime. Downtime guards against emotional overload, provided you do not use it as an excuse for making yourself unavailable. *Me* time is not a Get Out of Jail Free card for avoiding the other person's emotional needs but should be a recharging for meeting them.

Consider it this way, selfishness and selflessness, when in a healthy relationship, is a give-and-take proposition. It is not an all-or-nothing bet. It rests on compromise as much as it rests on consideration. Once you are willing to stop a minute and think of the other person, when you are able to examine your actions, you will be able to confidently hold a generous position with every relationship in your life.

It is not easy to change or correct a behavior as ingrained as the "I" mindset because it is taught from an early age. (No, this isn't about blaming your mother.) We are all taught early on to stand up for ourselves, to be confident, to speak up. And those are all good qualities to have. They have the tendency to become not-so-good qualities when we hold them too high.

Being a selfless person doesn't mean you cannot stand up or speak out or be confident. It simply means you need to be tuned in to the other person at the same time. Tweak the "I" mindset a little bit to allow for giving a little more generously to the other person.

Chapter Nine
Step Seven: Forgive and Ask for Forgiveness

Regardless of how healthy your relationship is with another person, there will be times it will spark a note—or even an entire chorus—of anger. The other person will do something or say something or not do something or not say something that will send you straight into a fit. And, like all those other times and other relationships, you are going to hold on to the pain you have suffered or the hurt you have endured or disappointment you have faced like a kid holding on to a favorite toy.

And before you say, "I am not," think about the last time a friend let you down. Maybe they forgot to pick you up from the airport or forgot about plans you had for seeing that new movie or never paid back that fifty dollars they borrowed or let you down over and over.

Whatever it was left you feeling disappointed and oh, maybe, (go on admit it) a little bit hurt.

Okay, did the friend apologize? Okay, did you forgive them? Oh, sure, you moved past the incident, but that is not the same as forgiving them. If you are still carrying around the disappointment and are still feeling a twinge of that hurt, no, you have not forgiven them. And heaven forbid the friend never apologized, or never apologized the way you felt was sufficient (expecting them to prostrate themselves in public before you, yes, would be too much to expect), you will, if even on some subconscious level, hold on to this until the day you die.

It is time to let it go. Oh sure, we've all heard the saying about life being too short and it all being small stuff. Honestly, life might be too short, but it's not always such small stuff. And what might be small stuff to somebody else might not be so small to you; however, that does not mean you need to hold it all the way to the grave.

The closer you are to another person, the more intimate a relationship is, the greater chance there is for disappointment and hurt. Be prepared for it. As a matter of fact, expect it. That's right, expect it. Be glad for it because it's only the closest of relationships that endure the deepest hurts.

You'd never flat out tell the new neighbor they look like they're gaining a little weight, but you'd have no problem telling your spouse to cut back on the chips, right? Yeah, you're laughing. Well, what if the new neighbor sent a little honesty your way? Sometimes the hurt we feel is not from an intimate source, making it all the more harder to forgive, and all the more important you forgive it.

Remember when you were a kid? Another kid did something that made you mad then almost immediately said, "Sorry, wanna be friends again?" You said, "Sure," and all was forgiven. Nothing has really changed except for how complicated we have now made it to forgive and to be forgiven.

Granted, you encounter more now than someone pulling the red fringe off your bicycle handlebars, but the concept remains the same. You need to be able to forgive and move on, and you need to be able to ask for forgiveness and move on. And you need to be able to do this with a true sense of being, that is to say without a defensive position.

You cannot take on a defensive position and still forgive someone any more than you can take on a defensive position and ask for forgiveness. And while there are a host of things which can conceivably be considered absolutely unforgivable, it is for your own well-being you need to forgive them just the same.

Understand, however, forgiving the hurt is not the same as forgiving the person. Maybe that kid repeatedly pulled the red fringe off the handlebars. It wouldn't matter how many times they said, "Sorry, wanna be friends again?" At some point, you'd say no and walk away because you'd recognize it's not a good friendship, it's an unhealthy relationship. With the next friend you have to move past your hurt.

That is the hard part. How do you forgive something and move past it when it has made you so darned mad? How do you ask for and give forgiveness? You start by foregoing your naturally defensive position.

You cannot apologize to someone and expect them to forgive you if you start with, "I'm sorry, but I only did it because . . ." nor can you forgive someone and expect them to believe you are sincere if you say, "I accept your apology, but . . ." Those are both defensive positions and they are both positions supported by pride, and you know where pride goeth, don't you?

It is fair to say most people have a hard time forgiving others and even asking for forgiveness because they have a difficult time forgiving themselves. You cannot possibly expect to exhibit the level of compassion in forgiveness to others if you cannot manage this for yourself.

Now maybe you are one of those incredibly ideal people, one of the rare gems who has nothing to forgive themselves for. Well, good for you! However, if you are like the rest of us mortals, you have plenty of guilt squashed deep down, and you need to find a way to make peace with it and let it go. You need to find a way to forgive your sins, and this starts by being contrite, which is not quite the same as being sorry.

The word *sorry* is thrown around with all the casual frequency of changing socks. You forgot to hang up your jacket; *oops, sorry.* You forgot to feed the dog; *oh, sorry.* You forgot to put gas in the car; *oh, yeah, sorry.* People don't pay attention when they say it anymore or when they hear it. There is no contrition behind it.

Some things need apologizing; others do not. It is important you know the difference and take responsibility accordingly. That is how you forgive yourself, that is how you forgive another person, and that is how you ask for forgiveness. You recognize the act and the intention. You don't have to like it, you can reserve the right to be mad, but you have to recognize it.

You have to learn to systematically break down the act from the intention and, more importantly, the person from the act. Was it a good friend, a close relationship who left you stranded at the airport? Then chances are there was no intention behind the act, and the contrition will come from the heart, which is no less how you should meet it.

If the friend was distant, a casual relationship, chances are the reverse is true, and the intention was deliberate to some degree, but, and this is the hard part, you still have to meet it with a true forgiveness. You don't have to trust that friend to depend on again, but you have to forgive their intent. If you cannot do this, you will allow it to slowly taint and tarnish your other relationships.

In short, people all tend to judge others by who or what has come before because, despite wanting to believe all that overpacked baggage is neatly stowed, you are probably still carrying it around and pulling it through all the other relationships in your life— including the one with yourself.

So start with yourself. Look at your own acts and intentions. Recognize which need apologizing for and which do not, and let them go. When you can do this, you will be able to look at the relationships in your life, forgive what needs to be forgiven, and ask for forgiveness for what needs forgiving.

Chapter Ten
Step Eight: Be Appreciative

We are all familiar with the phrase, "Little things mean a lot," right? It turns up in songs, in books, and in advertisements pushing everything from the latest celebrity perfume to old-fashioned ice cream. But do you know what it means? Do you get the concept?

So often, especially in long-held relationships, this concept is lost—or is at least somewhat off course. Think back to when you first met your spouse or your closest friend or that closest colleague at work. You were all about being thoughtful, weren't you? You did all sorts of things to show your appreciation for them. You brought home flowers for no reason or you always made sure the gas tank was full or you routinely picked up the tab for coffee. Yep, you did all the little things that mean so much. You did all those little things that made the other person feel really appreciated. You probably even made a habit of saying "please" and "thank you."But then time passed and the flowers got expensive and what did it matter if the gas tank wasn't on full, the car had gas, and the bills for those coffees really started to add up. And you don't need to be so polite with someone you're close with, it's so formal. Yes, all that might be true, but what's more true is you got comfortable. You got complacent and grew tired of doing those little things, so you just stopped doing them.

All right, maybe you did. It's no big deal, right? The other person still knew you cared, didn't they? Yeah, sure, if the other person is a certified mind reader they knew, but it's more likely they are just an ordinary person who was left feeling unappreciated, downright taken for granted, and what's more, disrespected.

Okay now, it's a big deal because people don't stay where they aren't appreciated or where they don't *feel* they are appreciated. Appreciation brings loyalty, and people will always eventually go where they feel appreciated and not just tolerated.

Consider for a minute if you had a great job, a dream job, the job of a lifetime. Maybe you are making more money than you can even spend, but the atmosphere is lousy. You have a boss who is all sorts of miserable and you are always being put upon to work a little longer or take on another project when you are already overloaded. You never hear the words "please" or "thank-you." How does that make you feel, a little unappreciated? A little disrespected? A little taken for granted? Would you stay? Yes, all right, maybe for a while, but eventually you will leave. You will seek out someplace where maybe the money is not so great but the *emotional* self-worth is merited.

When you take the time to extend some small gesture to show the other person you appreciate them, that you appreciate what they do for you, you benefit as much as the other person because thoughtfulness is reciprocal. And by comparison, so is your failing to extend these small gestures. Be it good or bad, you will get back what you put out.

When you act as if what you are asking the other person to do is expected, when you act as if you are entitled to them doing it for you, you take on an air of superiority; you demean the other person's self-worth. You don't mean it, of course, but that is how you are coming across and, except for the certified mind readers, the other person is not going to know what you mean; they are going to know only what you show.

If you say to your spouse, "I'm running late, I left my shirt for you to iron." You might as well say, "Iron this, servant, and make it fast." The initial statement (and by the way, using the latter is not advised) will probably get your shirt ironed, but it will also bring on an argument, hurt feelings, and a full-length discussion about not being a servant, provided you didn't toss the shirt in their general direction when you asked them.

If you have a big project at work you can't seem to get through, don't tell your colleague they "have" to help you; ask them if they wouldn't mind "please" giving you a hand. And in return, be thoughtful; make an effort to show your appreciation. Bring home your spouse's favorite candy bar, or treat your colleague to lunch. Let the other person know the things they do matter, let them know *they* matter.

Everyone wants to feel appreciated, respected, and even needed, but when you put your own needs ahead of the other person's feelings, all they feel is hurt. Your actions will not only speak louder than your words, your actions will be reciprocated. "Do unto others" is not just for Bible study. Do you want to be treated like you matter above all else? Then treat the other person as if they do. If you want the other person to do things for you, then do things for the other person.

However, do not treat favors as if they have price tags. Do not keep score for cashing in at some later date. Showing appreciation is not a quid pro quo act. In fact, it is the exact opposite. When you do something for someone, expect nothing in return. And when something is done for you, do not feel obligated to bestow some trinket on the other person *every* time. That completely undermines the entire concept. Ask politely, respond in kind, and let reciprocity come naturally.

Keep it simple, keep it real, and do as your mother taught you and mind your manners.

Chapter Eleven
Staying the Course

Have you ever had one of those days? Or have you ever said to yourself: there has to be more to my life than this? What to do? Quite honestly, sometimes there is nothing *to* do. There are times when the best thing you can do is nothing but let the situation play out.

The same holds true for relationships. Sometimes, despite your best efforts, despite your doing and saying all the right things, the relationship is just doomed, and nothing you do is going to change that because there will be times when it is not you; it is the other person.

So how do you not let this affect you? How do you go through the crash and burn of a relationship and get back on course? How do you muster enough energy to push forward and build and maintain other healthy relationships?

To tell you the truth, it's not easy. There is nothing more exhausting than managing a crisis, and there is almost nothing more exhausting than a failed relationship. It is exhausting. It can take everything out of you—if you let it.

Even if the relationship is to survive, getting through the crisis can be traumatic. Of course, not every situation is a crisis and not every crisis is critical; you need to know and understand the difference because while how you manage each one is relatively the same, how you manage the relationship with the other person is definitely not.

Managing a situation, be it a crisis or not, is entirely different than managing the relationship with the other person. To manage the situation you need to assess and process. You assess the facts and you process your course of action. You can utilize a nonemotional response, which is not to say you don't feel anything. You have to develop more of a calm, cool, and collected mindset.

Now, managing the relationship with the other person in a given situation is a different horse of a different color because no matter how masterful you are at assessing and processing, the other person might not have read this book and is going to be managing on a completely different, and very emotionally charged, level.

For example, let's say you are fired from a well-paying job. You have a spouse, a family, a mortgage, and savings enough for maybe six months. No matter how healthy your relationship is, it is about to hit a major curve and possibly a wall.

Your spouse will likely be supportive . . . at first, but the bills are going to start coming in as fast as the money is going out, and what at first is a stressful situation is about to become a full crisis . . . again, if you let it.

What to do? First, manage the situation. Assess the facts, and not the obvious no job, no money facts. You are already assessing those and processing them by sending out resumes, going on interviews, pounding the pavement. No, you need to assess the more relevant underlying facts. You have a spouse who is scared or even angry, and you have a family in distress. This, not a job, is your primary concern; this is your primary focus. You need to do serious crisis management and repair the damage if you are to maintain a healthy relationship.

How do you do this? This is where managing the relationship with the other person comes in. You cannot make less of their emotions. Whether or not their emotions are valid is irrelevant. What is relevant is your being able, your being willing, to acknowledge them. This is key in diffusing an emotional explosion.

Once you have done that, you can then manage the situation. Many times people retreat in stressful situations. They battle internally and tough it out. But while you are toughing it out, what invariably happens is resentment grows and builds so even after the situation is past, your resentment is already rooted. Your seemingly healthy relationship has been critically weakened.

An adverse situation, even a crisis, does not always cause a relationship to collapse. It can sometimes strengthen a relationship, but you have to know how to manage it. You have to be able to know and understand what can be saved, what cannot be saved, and more importantly, the difference between these two because that is how you will determine what is worth saving.

And while it would be nice to think every relationship is worth saving, it is not so. Sometimes a relationship is temporary, it is not intended to be permanent, and nothing you do is going to change that.

When a relationship or situation ends without warning, you immediately want to know what happened, right? Of course you do. You have a need to understand what happened. What you need to understand, however, is more important than understanding what happened. That is the lesson that relationship taught you and, yes, without getting philosophical, *every* relationship in our life—be it temporary or long term—teaches a lesson. From the kid who pulled the red fringe off our bicycle handlebars to the miserable boss to our oldest friend or our wonderful spouse (and even the two who came before), every one of those relationships brought a lesson into our life, and all those lessons lined up to give us the wherewithal to build and maintain healthy relationships.

Chapter Twelve
Embrace the Changes

Well, my friend, there you have it, the tools for building and maintaining healthy relationships. Can you now be assured of light and balance in your life with never a dark cloud overhead? Can you now rest easy, never to be bothered by the slings and arrows of discord? Can you now expect songbirds to greet you at the start of each morning? Unless you are planning a move to some other realm far away from reality, no, I am afraid not.

Wait. Before you rush back to the bookstore for a refund, let me tell you what you can be assured of. First off, you wouldn't want any of the above because as idealistic as it sounds, it would be stifling. How would you grow? From what would you learn? Good days are nice, they are wonderful, and you should strive for them and work toward them, but don't underestimate the bad days. Without them there would be nothing to appreciate.

Second, while I cannot predict all moonlight and roses for you, if you implement these practices into your daily life, what I can predict for you is a change, a change in yourself and in those around you.

It will start slowly. There will be setbacks and backsliding, but you will pick yourself up and carry forward because you are now working toward the greater good, the better you. You will find, in small ways at first, a more enriched life, and no, this does not mean you will grow rich. Your life will be enriched, *enhanced,* at first by a deepened understanding of who you are and an improved, *healthier* relationship with yourself.

Each step you have taken here will lead you to live a truer and more genuine life so the bad days, and there will still be bad days, will be manageable. By practicing and putting into practice what you have learned, you will manage your life, not the other way around.

Does this mean you will *feel* different? Yes, on some levels, but don't look for some sudden epiphany to strike, and don't look for your life or other people to change. They won't. You will. You will change the way you look at your life, and you will make changes where changes need to be made. You will look at who is in your life and question *why*. Do they have a deserved place, or are they a placeholder filling a gap? You will look at the choices and decisions you have made with a healthier vision for where you are going. You will be able to recognize your path, your own road to happiness.

On that road there will be bumps, there will be stops, there will even be the occasional accident. It doesn't mean the road is dead-ended. It means you need to re*assess*. Take a step back and *process* the situation. Remember those two tools? You have lived your entire life up until this point going one way in one direction on one road with one vision. The view now is changed; the road now is new. You need to breathe and allow yourself to become aware of your new environment. Enjoy it, revel in it, and take it all in with a child's delight.

Children might question where they are going, but
for the most part they are just happy to go. Yes, all
right, they question a thousand times if they are there
yet, but they haven't read this book. You have, so you
know better.

This is a joy ride as much as it is a journey of self-
discovery. Don't be afraid to ask yourself questions.
How else can you learn? Don't be afraid to make
changes. How else can you grow?

Yes, I know. Change is hard, even a little scary.
(We have covered that already.) But change is only
hard or scary the first time. After that it's the start of
a routine, a new and healthier routine. Give yourself
time to adjust and settle in, and you might just find
mornings a little bit better, even without the songbirds.

Okay, so much for the upside to using your new
tools. What about the downside? And, much as I would
like to tell you otherwise, there is a downside and
here it is: you will need to evaluate your relationships
and consider phasing out those that no longer have a
genuine place. This will be the hardest change and
the most crucial if you expect to maintain healthy
relationships.

You simply cannot keep an unhealthy relationship and expect it to not impact a healthy relationship on some level, and unfortunately it seldom works the other way around. It's like chocolate cake and carrots. A giant bowl of carrots chock full of vitamins and good healthy nutrients can be entirely overridden by one innocent-looking piece of chocolate cake. And no, glazing the carrots and drowning them in butter does not make them even.

Okay, I trust it is safe to say you get it now, yes? You are ready to peel away all those well-worn layers you've built up over the years and take a good long, hard look at yourself. Start easy, go slow, like that earlier skiing lesson. Don't head straight for the black diamond trail; tackle the bunny hill first.

A word of caution as you embark on this new journey: be careful when sharing your newly found wisdom with others. You don't need all sorts of well-meaning, or not so well-meaning, friends (and even family) chiming in with their own version of what you need to do, should do, need to correct, should correct, and how to do it. Chances are these are the very "experts" who could use a copy of this book.

And while we are on this topic, don't brag or preach, either. You didn't get here all by yourself, and your being here doesn't make you perfect and doesn't make *you* an expert. Don't be looking to fix anybody else's life because you are still a work in progress and have a long way to go.

Focus on taking care of yourself and taking care of your relationships, and trust the rest will take care of itself. Generally speaking, when one aspect of your life is changed, so too are others—be it for the better or for the worse. Every aspect affects every other aspect. They are all connected. By changing one thing, you invariably will change the others. Alter one relationship and you alter the others.

However, you needn't make all the changes to all your relationships all at once. Seriously, please don't; the results would be disastrous. This isn't a race. You don't get extra points for completing the course in record time. Stay on the bunny hill awhile. It is not as easy as the bunnies make it look.

Listen, here's the basic bottom line: there will always be outside influences in your life. They will come from intimate relationships and distant acquaintances. They will be both useful and harmful, and they will be constant. Implementing the lessons you have been taught, you should now be able to decipher which of these influences is necessary and which are a nuisance. You should be able to recognize which serve a purpose and which are a distraction. And above all else, you should now be able to build and maintain healthy relationships in all aspects of your life.

Epilogue

In case you are left now to wonder who I am to be offering anybody advice, I will tell you straight up; I am no expert. What's more, not even the self-proclaimed experts are experts. While I do have a master's degree in psychology, this does not necessarily qualify me as an expert. So why listen to me? Why trust that any of this advice is worth the price of this book? What does make me qualified to offer advice to anybody on changing his or her life and relationships?

All fair questions, and I will give you a simple, direct, and straight answer. I am not an expert on anything other than my own experiences, and that is what I am offering you. What I have lived, what I have learned is no less than what I have laid out in the steps outlined in the previous chapters. It is core advice drawn from a lot of long and hard years. Advice gathered from hard experiences spent living on the rough side of life and surviving the pains and hurts to where the scars formed and faded to leave ingrained patterns for building and maintaining healthy relationships with others in my life. There is singularly no better teacher than experience.

Do I make it sound easy? Believe me, it wasn't. It was a long and hard road and it takes a lot of day-to-day work still. Do I ever drop the ball? Of course I do. I am not perfect, I am human, and I am still learning. But I have learned enough about myself to recognize when I have dropped the ball, and I can recognize when I need to pick the ball back up and get back in the game. That is key; you must be able to manage your own failings and keep moving forward.

It is a bit like that first time you rode a bike without the training wheels. You were all over the place trying to keep your balance. How many mail posts did you run into? How many trees did you hit before you managed to keep it steady? It isn't really so different now. Now you just have to learn a new balance, a balance to your life. And while I don't expect you to run into any mail posts or trees (unless you are reading this book while walking, in which case I take no responsibility), I do expect you will likely run into a few roadblocks. These are the same roadblocks put up by *you* years ago. Move them; you do not need them. Be prepared, though, for moving them to be an arduous task, but you *can* do it. You are ready. It's like riding a bike: once you manage your balance, you move forward without wobbling, without thinking. It just takes some time and practice.

That is what it will take now, time and practice. Take it one step at a time. Find your balance, go slowly, and get the feel of it. Have fun with it, explore each new step, and take the time to really look at what you will discover. After awhile you won't stop and think about it, you will just go with it. The steps will take you where you need to be.

I have not pretended with you, and I am not about to start now. This is a lifelong process. Yes, it will get easier, as with anything you do over time, but it will never end for the mere fact there will always be challenges and obstacles in life to deal with. And no two days, no two situations, and no two relationships will ever be exactly alike, so do not expect to be able to manage them in exactly the same way.

There are only two certainties in life: you were born, and you will die. Other than that, it is all up for grabs, so you need to be able to keep up. That is all this book can allow for, helping you keep up, helping you *manage*. Please do not expect anything more, and above all else, please do not expect this book or these steps to make for your having an easy life. *You* are the only one who can arrange that. What this book, what these eight steps can do, if you trust enough to follow them, is maybe make for an easier way for you to manage the relationships in your life, but you do have to *want* it. Deep down, you have to really want it; you have to be willing to really work at it every day. If not, no amount of time and practice will matter.

Implement what you have learned here—all of it. No selective learning. You don't get to pick and choose the steps, which you like, which you don't, which you'll follow, and which you won't. Even though it rhymed, it doesn't work that way. You are either in or you are out for this journey. Are you ready?

Okay, well, we have come to the part now where you have a choice, and it is your choice. You can continue on the same road you have been on for all these years doing all the same things in the same way and you will pretty well get all the same results. And if you are happy with that, that's okay. But you *did* buy the book, so maybe, deep down, some small part of you isn't all that happy. Maybe you know there are changes that need to be made for building and managing good healthy relationships with others in your life.

Consider that a minute—building and managing healthy relationships with others in your life. Imagine how much better this will make you feel.

www.ingramcontent.com/pod-product-compliance
Lightning Source LLC
Chambersburg PA
CBHW060954040426
42445CB00011B/1149